FORTUNATELY

FORTUNATELY

poems

Nava EtShalom

—

Published by Button Poetry / Exploding Pinecone Press

Minneapolis, MN 55403 | http://www.buttonpoetry.com

—

For Yonah

CONTENTS

FORTUNATELY

BEFORE THE BIRDS

I did—on the mountainside—tell him
we loved him, and God did, and tied

his hands behind his back, wide palms, tapered fingers,
with a local rope I had been keeping for just this occasion.

He liked the rope like I like a snug jacket, like he once liked
to sit in someone's lap. He liked the knife like we all like

to know finally we've been right: this is a disaster
and the end, thank God and the overcast morning, has come.

We'll do it how we do it. We'll stay with you
from death until the burial, the song, the empty trees.

RECOGNITION

I'll cede ground that isn't mine.
I'll make my grandparents' apologies,
I'll make my own, since they're still here
taking constitutionals, surveying. Even
my renunciations are cribbed.
We think we own our graves

on the Mount of Olives, graves
in the hills beyond Jerusalem, doorbells
along the old streets where my name appears,
and at the corner somebody surprises me
wearing my face. Who's to say whose.
Here's capital and all its homelessness.

We've paid for our graves up front
with a view of the messiah. We're living
in the waiting room. I've changed
the allegiance of my plural pronoun, given up
my primordial lisp. A great theft made me, and now
this is no place for family life.

BEGATS

Exaltation of larks, bloat
of patriarchs, series
of serious butches: series
of serious books: an aquarian
palette: a rage jacket:
a shine that never
wears off: headscarves,
signatures, a late announcement:
an octave: age: absentia:
the ax, its mirrored edge:
one palmed key: the second
time: if anything, fire:

ARRIVAL

On the ship's manifest, there are matches
and maps wrapped against the weather;
blankets, boots, hooks of all sizes—

for grappling, for fish, for fastening.
Pencils, soap, gunpowder,
envelopes and lengths of chain.

Powdered milk and cured olives, all
the knives we'll need. Skirts as thin
as nothing, subject to the wind. Everyone

arrives silent at the rails. Some hands, some
rescued palms to palms, some barely kept
from leaping over. As night

sets in, bread and salt, we watch the land,
the tall candles burning welcome. Those are only gulls
shaped like us, waiting on the rocks.

MATERIALS

Gave a heart to fire, preferred
the hollow chest, filled

two hands with my body—
back-to-chest, palm-to-hip.

Two forgotten countries
carried on with local plans—

I never made anything
but a concession to thunder.

GOD OF SUICIDES

I have been wrong before, god of syntax
and understatement, god of slips in silk
and polyester, god of the laboratory, god of newsprint
and sunscreen, god of gulls, god of the unlocked bakery,
god of twins, god of all the cities of my youngest years,
god of the nurses who walk those wards, god
of sensible shoes and of Wall Street, god of whales
and their depths, god of the kitchen, god
of the blood clot, god of the authoritative sentence,
god of weight and liquor, god of scarves
and of the required fast, god of the green room
and the downbeat, god of lemons,
god of the disappeared and god of their mothers,
god of the highway's meridian, god
of all 206 bones and the compulsive catalogue,
god of freckles, god of rhinoplasty, god of narcotics, god
of the Five-Year Plan, god of the solemn
and the sudden, god of the stage,
god of runways, god of release on one's own
recognizance, god of the unrecognized face, god
of divorce and of lip gloss, god of crosswalks
and alphabets, god of M16s
and god of hands without instructions,
god of attention, god of the tucked
chin, god of the article,
god of the attitude, god of direction, god
of the rowhome and its master bedroom,

god of the pinstriped suit, the knuckles,
but in all of these furious declamatory years the question
has never been, god of what, god of the city's brick,
god of my palm, god of my open mouth.

HOLY COMMITTEE

We cut it down from the taut rope, you and I, we
checked its pockets for a name, we prepared it
for the clean white cloth. We took its thin
clothes off, but that was not enough, nor was the
careful bath, nor the laying-out on old tile, nor
our hands over its eyes, our warm skin, my
fingers notched between your teeth, your jaw
fastened around my shoulder's bones. None of
us were ready. The sun began anyway to set into
the low kitchen window, the moon making a late
arrival. The moon is not a person. The rock is
not a moon, the years it took to release my arm
from yours is not an allegory, it is the body
dissolving, the way we look at once smoother
and older in the evening, in our private mirrors.
It was a dark afternoon, but something brightened
in the city and the body, head unspeakable, toes in
the soup, turned into view.

LANDING

In Jerusalem a dead phone's dialed by exiles.
—*Agha Shahid Ali*

1

In a litany of safer places, we name hospitals,
highways, runways, where a body

is at least in motion. Sticking
hard to its own fable,

something simple about linen
and penmanship. The whole heart's

at work there, drawing dirt
from a garden of artichokes

for the eventual burial, far
from home, against a quiet sky.

2

The body and its constituent bones cross
dark oceans. These have names
and envelop the globe. Still

they are standing in. Its smells
and inconstancies, its unwilled dissolutions,
leave our hands empty, leave our hands.

3

Our bodies go down
unwrapped, or all in white.

BEGATS II

The bargain bin of used
books, the accompanying
cassette tape, the nightmare
of being pulped: three
women's voices in close
harmony: a circle of tall pines:
the zip of tape pulled
from its reel: new potatoes,
radishes, sprouted alfalfa: haircuts
we'll regret later, haircuts
we won't even admit to
later: cascading
failures of irony, cascading
failures of warmth: an industrial
kitchen and its industrial
ingredients: poster board,
the fattest markers
from the pile: all the deaths
we sidestepped, the electric hearths
we warmed, and dirt.

CERTAINLY

The call is bad news, both dogs are panting, the afternoon
is punctuated by sudden sleep, I hang a navy dress by the shower
which does nothing to shake its wrinkles out, and I mind

as if the dead mind. Or we have fish on Fridays—
in this version I seem to be Catholic—or
only my richest friend survives the wreck, or I count the funerals

I will and won't fan myself at, weep tidily through, cry
too loud at, be dead before, or that was the only love I had
after all, and all other loves paled next to it, or

the semblance of democracy gave out and we scrambled
for what food was left, in cans—what water,
caught in tarps—or I never saw 36, or 27, or adulthood

fizzled too quickly into age, and I kept putting off my suicide
to spare my mother's feelings, procrastinated
until I stood at her grave with dirt from Jerusalem in my fist,

redeemed from statehood, and we reminded each other
to throw, or we have cultivated imagination and hopelessness
in heaps and spades, and where have they gotten us.

GENERATION

In the coven that raised me
nobody considered silence. All mysteries

were mysteries of speech. All questions
were questions of the mouth.

We raged against ellipsis. Tuesdays
we restored the book of names.

Here I am, I tell them now, cleaving
to the mean lyric, pouring tea.

I've talked myself hoarse—fig, cracker—
and all I am is—honey—exegesis.

PROPOSAL

The promise of gravel, one skinned
arm and turned knee,
one bicycle and its wheels:

The chin-up of light,
morning gift in pine, this space
my palms describe:

The excellent refraction inside
whiskey, that unassailable place
we live within liquid:

The belly-up of fish all morning
on that morbid walk after
the tides have given up:

Those good citizens, the trees
and their branches, leaves that uncurl even
into our hostile spring:

The gazelle and its sister,
a gazelle; the other names for deer, ticked off
on our fingers:

The tent and the place we lived
inside it, two feet by two, and your hands
across my belly like lightning:

RECOVERY

You're a runoff pipe, an empty
apartment, a vacuum, so of course
the stars rush through you. You're soaked

in oxygen, your dreams and nightmares
go sea-skimming. Secret enemies
line up along linoleum hallways,

a sponge bath on an electric panel, travel
from the Pleistocene to the age of plastic.
Open your mouth.

ITERATION

Knowing what I know, I still want

children. Two, with complementary

rages. Deep fjords

through the heart. This side

of the backseat, that side, the life

and the death of me:

one holy committee, one terror.

BEGATS III

A thumbprint lake
on someone else's land:
shame: a wall's flakes, stone
and drywall and plaster:
temporary homes made
from wood and rope: scribes
and reliquaries: a matching
gap: gasoline: everything
we offered to the air.

UNFORTUNATELY

This side of the mountain's turning
toward night and the green blazes have faded,

I'm supposed to be the calm one, your hand
when I hold it warms me through, we have never been

enough company, you buried the keys
with dog zeal and I wish you'd like me less,

it's a series of left turns, when the house comes into view
it's the wrong one after all. All my bets have been bad bets.

EARTHQUAKE

Cliffside where the rhyme
is nearly visible: red mud
and the red wall thinned out

to an orange in my nail bed
and the delicate skin behind your ears.
When I open my eyes again

to a new sound, it's green and the world
is reassembling itself, stratum
of earth by stratum of pearl.

CHARISMA

I'm more Mosaic every week: virtuously
burned, slow of speech. My brother
speaks for me. I am a brutalizer
of the brutalizer, a pillar of correctness
following a pillar of smoke and a pillar
of fire. I am slow of speech. I'll go
to the top of the mountain alone
for my epiphany, for my glimpse
of all the murderers and orchardists
to come, whom I have been defending
all these years under whatever laws
I can remember with my unbearable
face, that was young when we began.

NOTES

Landing: This epigraph comes from a poem Agha Shahid Ali published as "Ghazal 1" and dedicated to Edward Said in the Fall 1997 issue of *Triquarterly*. It appeared later without the dedication and with an epigraph from Mahmoud Darwish, first as "Ghazal" in *Rooms are Never Finished* and later as "By Exiles" in the posthumous collection *Call Me Ishmael Tonight*. The epigraph that appears in later editions is from Darwish's "The Earth is Closing In On Us."

Proposal: "Those good citizens, the trees" come from *Trees As Good Citizens*, a book housed at the Prelinger Library in San Francisco that was a prop in a 2008 contest run by the Third Coast Festival.

ACKNOWLEDGEMENTS

Thanks to the editors of the journals where several of these poems first appeared: *The Believer*, *Blackbird*, *The American Poetry Review*, and *Boston Review*.

I'm grateful to Hanif Abdurraqib, Sam Van Cook, and Hitomi Wong at Button Poetry for their great care in making this book and for working with me while I figured things out as a newly disabled poet.

Thanks to Ragdale, Hedgebrook, Willapa Bay AiR, and the Pew Fellowships in the Arts for generous support and beautiful hospitality during the writing of some of these poems. Thanks to the Grind, too, where some of them were first drafted.

Thanks to Amy Kaplan, who teaches me boldness and precision.

Thanks to my favorite poet-collaborator, Elizabeth Gramm, and to Jessica Hurley, fellow traveler extraordinaire.

And finally, love and gratitude to my family, friends, and circles of mutual aid. Thank you for the ways you say, in private and in public, that we are all lovable and all grievable.

ABOUT THE AUTHOR

Nava EtShalom's poems have appeared in *The American Poetry Review*, *Boston Review*, *The Believer*, and other journals. Her poetry has won the 92Y Discovery Prize, a Pew Fellowship in the Arts, and prizes from the Academy of American Poets. She has an MFA in poetry from the University of Michigan and is a doctoral candidate in English at the University of Pennsylvania, where she writes about literary representations of settler-colonialism in Palestine.

OTHER BOOKS BY BUTTON POETRY

If you enjoyed this book, please consider checking out some of
our others, below. Readers like you allow us to keep
broadcasting and publishing. Thank you!

Neil Hilborn, *Our Numbered Days*
Hanif Abdurraqib, *The Crown Ain't Worth Much*
Olivia Gatwood, *New American Best Friend*
Donte Collins, *Autopsy*
Melissa Lozada-Oliva, *peluda*
Sabrina Benaim, *Depression & Other Magic Tricks*
William Evans, *Still Can't Do My Daughter's Hair*
Rudy Francisco, *Helium*
Guante, *A Love Song, A Death Rattle, A Battle Cry*
Rachel Wiley, *Nothing Is Okay*
Neil Hilborn, *The Future*
Phil Kaye, *Date & Time*
Andrea Gibson, *Lord of the Butterflies*
Blythe Baird, *If My Body Could Speak*
Desireé Dallagiacomo, *SINK*
Dave Harris, *Patricide*
Michael Lee, *The Only Worlds We Know*
Raych Jackson, *Even the Saints Audition*
Brenna Twohy, *Swallowtail*
Porsha Olayiwola, *i shimmer sometimes, too*
Jared Singer, *Forgive Yourself These Tiny Acts of Self-Destruction*
Adam Falkner, *The Willies*
Kerrin McCadden, *Keep This To Yourself*
George Abraham, *Birthright*
Omar Holmon, *We Were All Someone Else Yesterday*
Rachel Wiley, *Fat Girl Finishing School*

Available at buttonpoetry.com/shop and more!